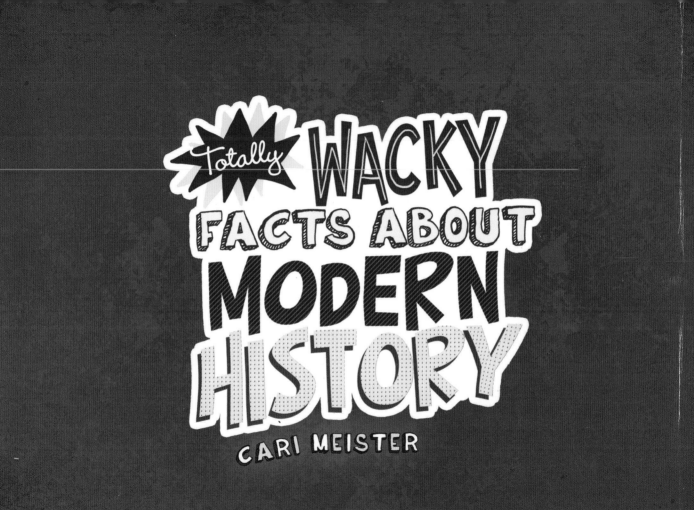

Totally WACKY FACTS ABOUT MODERN HISTORY

CARI MEISTER

raintree
a Capstone company — publishers for children

QUEEN ELIZABETH I
of England had more than 2,000 dresses.

In 1571 Queen Elizabeth I decreed that **ALL MEN HAD TO WEAR HATS ON SUNDAYS.**

Elizabeth I is the only English queen who never married.

A **HORDE** OF **RABBITS** ONCE ATTACKED THE FRENCH EMPEROR **NAPOLEON BONAPARTE.**

Napoleon suffered from **AILUROPHOBIA.** That means he was afraid of cats.

Napoleon didn't like his wife's name (Rose), so he changed it (to Josephine).

WINSTON CHURCHILL,

former prime minister of
GREAT BRITAIN,
was related to George Washington,
the first US president.

Churchill loved his bed so much, he often
held important meetings in his bedroom.

Churchill preferred **SLIP-ON SHOES** because he didn't like to waste time tying shoelaces.

ADOLF HITLER,

leader of Nazi Germany, was rejected from art school twice.

Hitler was so worried about being poisoned that he employed "food testers".

Hitler came up with the idea behind the **VOLKSWAGEN BEETLE.**

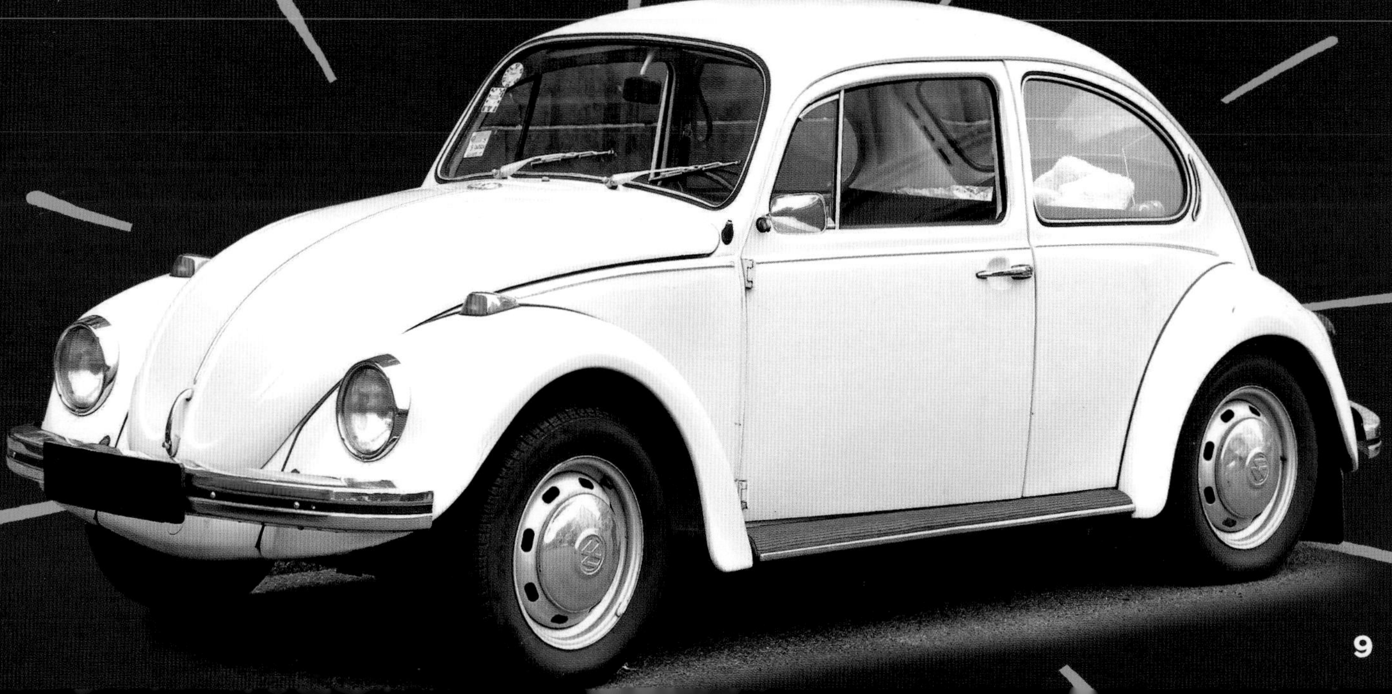

The famous magician **HARRY HOUDINI'S** first performance took place when he was just **9 YEARS OLD.**

In his first performance, Houdini picked up pins with his EYELASHES!

He made 25 pence for the performance.

When the pioneer pilot **AMELIA EARHART** was young, she had an imaginary Arabian horse named Saladin.

Earhart had her own aviation-inspired fashion line. It included blouses with propeller-shaped buttons.

In 1937 Amelia Earhart and her aeroplane disappeared over the Pacific Ocean.

GENGHIS KHAN

(1162–1227)
LEADER OF THE MONGOL EMPIRE

Genghis Khan conquered more than 31 million square kilometres (12 million square miles) of territory.

That's more than any other leader in history.

His death is a mystery.

Genghis Khan's legacy lives on – 16 million direct descendants carry his genes today.

The famous Italian artist and inventor
LEONARDO DA VINCI
drew plans for "floating snowshoes".

Da Vinci could draw with one hand at the same time his other hand wrote backwards.

Da Vinci was a very slow painter, and many of his paintings were never finished.

The famous physicist **ALBERT EINSTEIN** didn't start talking until he was 3 years old.

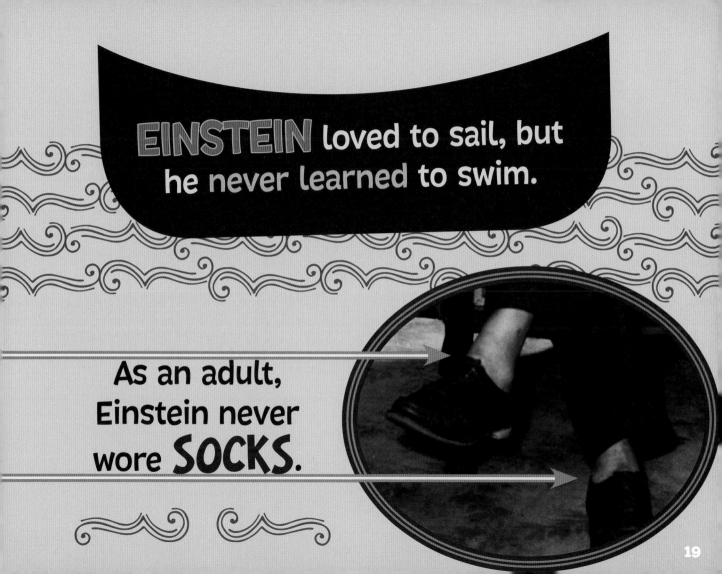

EINSTEIN loved to sail, but he never learned to swim.

As an adult, Einstein never wore **SOCKS**.

19

WOLFGANG MOZART, a famous composer, wrote music before he could write words.

MOZART wrote an entire symphony when he was only 8 years old.

Mozart's full name was

JOHANNES CHRYSOSTOMUS WOLFGANGUS THEOPHILUS MOZART.

AND NOW SOME WACKY FACTS ABOUT US PRESIDENTS:

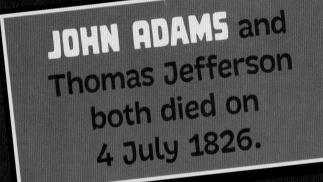

JOHN ADAMS and Thomas Jefferson both died on 4 July 1826.

ULYSSES S. GRANT once got a speeding ticket for riding his horse too fast.

CALVIN COOLIDGE often had people rub Vaseline on his head while he ate breakfast in bed.

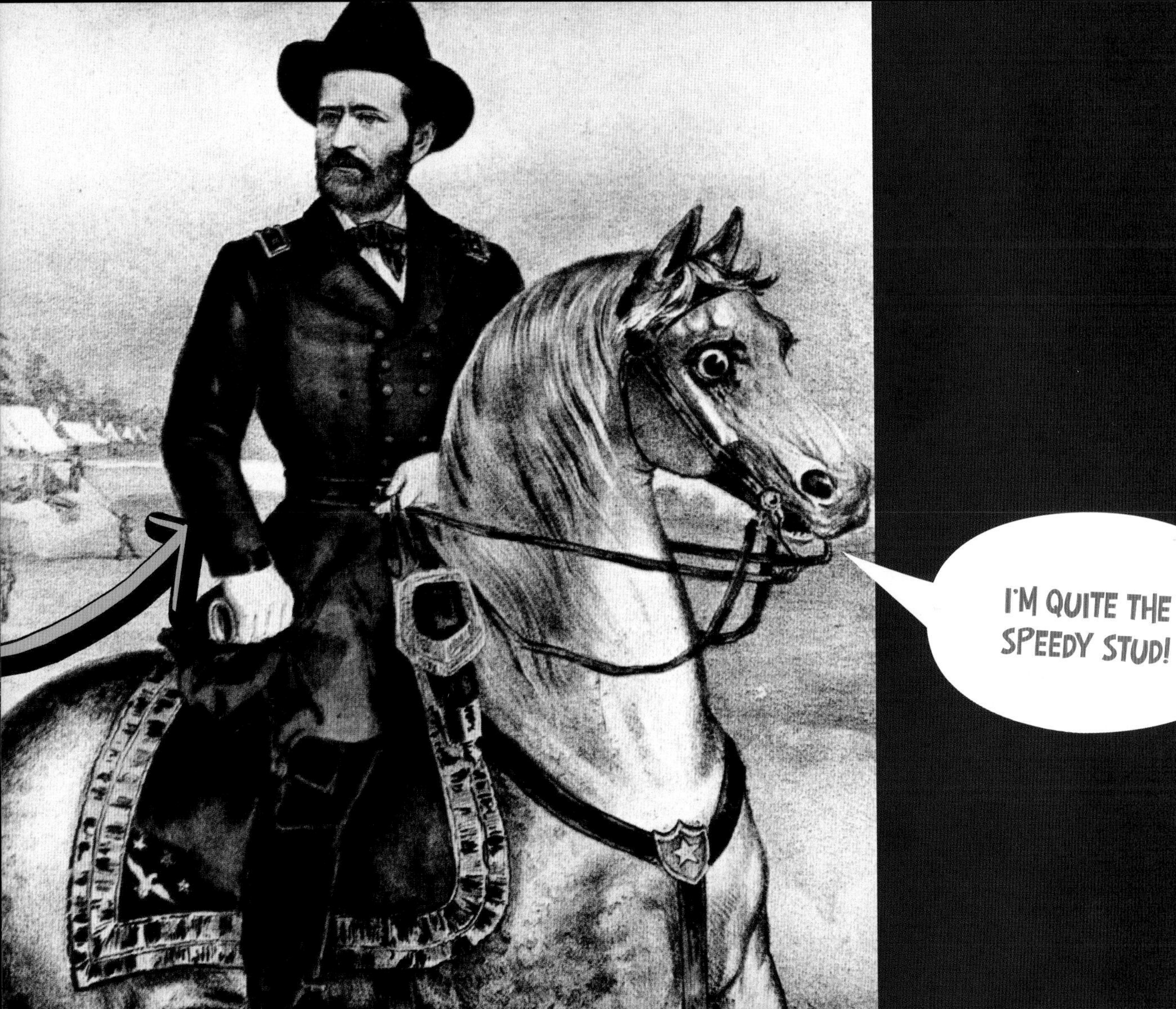
I'M QUITE THE SPEEDY STUD!

WOODROW WILSON painted his golf balls black so he could play in the snow.

The "S" in **HARRY S TRUMAN** does not stand for anything.

Six presidents have had the **first name** JAMES.

AND EVEN MORE ABOUT US PRESIDENTS:

HERBERT HOOVER'S first job was picking bugs off potato plants.

A family of plants was named after **THOMAS JEFFERSON.**

ABRAHAM LINCOLN was a licensed barman.

Most pirates didn't make captives **"WALK THE PLANK".** They just threw them overboard.

BLACKBEARD'S pirate ship was found off the coast of North Carolina, USA, in 1996. The ship was loaded with cannons.

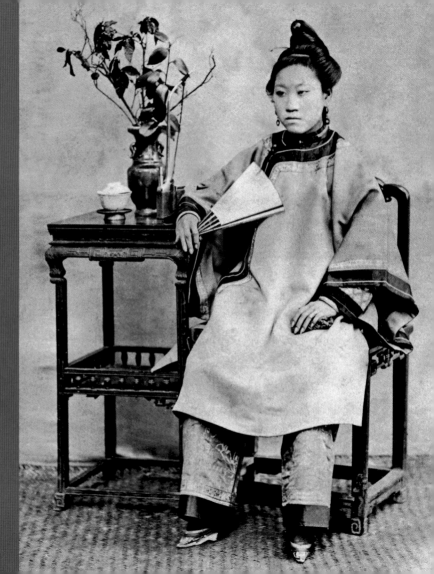

SMALL FEET

were considered **beautiful** in China, so parents would "bind" a daughter's feet to stunt their growth.

Some Europeans used to paint fake veins on their faces to make them look pale.

People used to whiten their skin with lead, which made their hair fall out.

WACKY HAIRSTYLES

"The Beehive", circa the 1950s

Japanese samurai "Chronmage", circa 12th–19th centuries

I just wish the bees WEREN'T SO LOUD.

32

Monks "Tonsure", circa 5th–15th centuries

"The Hedgehog", circa 1776

33

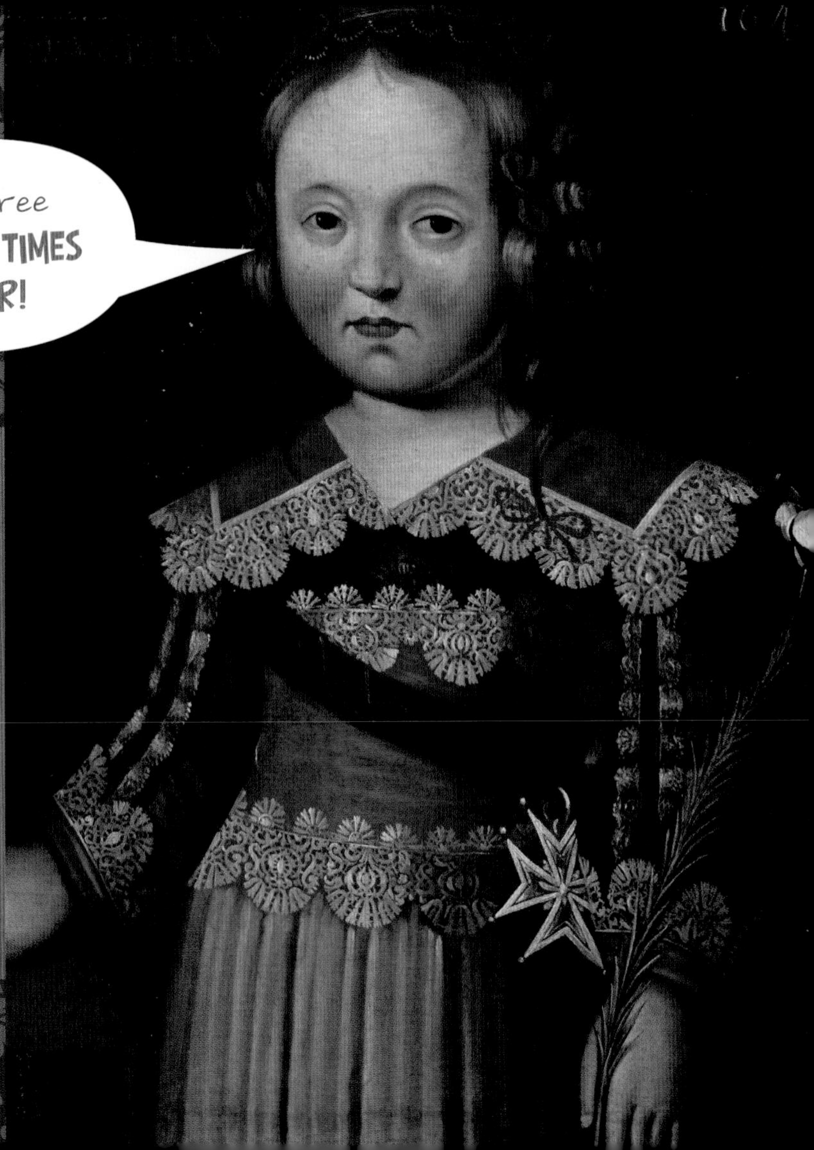

LOUIS XIV

was 4 years old when he became king of France.

MARY, QUEEN OF SCOTS, became queen when her father died. She was 6 days old!

PU-YI, the last emperor of China, came to power when he was 2 years old.

SULTAN ISMAIL of Morocco (1672–1727) had more than 1,000 children!

I bet he won't REMEMBER ALL OUR BIRTHDAYS!

An **18th century** Russian woman had **69 CHILDREN!**

16 PAIRS OF TWINS

7 SETS OF TRIPLETS

AND

4 SETS OF QUADRUPLETS

WORLD WAR I (1914–1918):

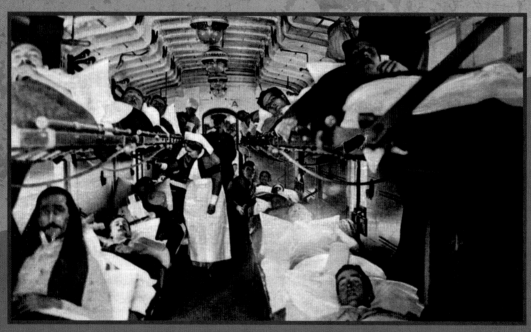

When Germans ran out of linen for bandages, they used lace curtains instead.

SPIES WROTE MESSAGES ON THE BACKS OF BUTTONS.

On CHRISTMAS DAY, 1914, GERMAN and BRITISH soldiers STOPPED FIGHTING and played FOOTBALL together.

WORLD WAR I (1914-1918):

TANKS were originally called "landships".

The **BRITISH** used the word "**TANK**" to **TRICK** their enemies into **THINKING** the vehicles were only **WATER TANKS**.

The first **SUBMARINE** was called **"THE TURTLE"** and was used in the **AMERICAN REVOLUTIONARY WAR.**

During the **REVOLUTIONARY WAR, GEORGE WASHINGTON** called a ceasefire to return his enemy's **LOST DOG.**

MYTHS ABOUT US PRESIDENT GEORGE WASHINGTON, EXPOSED!

His dentures were **NOT MADE OF WOOD**. They were made from a **combination** of **HIPPO IVORY** and **HORSE**, **HUMAN** and **DONKEY TEETH**.

HE NEVER CUT DOWN A CHERRY TREE.

THROUGHOUT HISTORY,
MANY THINGS WERE USED TO MAKE FALSE TEETH.

INCLUDING:

WOOD

ROCKS

IVORY

SEASHELLS

BONE

ANIMAL TEETH

From the
MEDIEVAL
Gross Files

People in medieval Europe drank
GOLD POWDER
mixed with water to relieve
sore muscles.

Wouldn't you rather have **CHERRY PIE??**

A medieval feast might include **"BLACKBIRD PIE"** or vulture.

49

The Chinese invented **TOILET PAPER** in the year 851 AD.

Other things people have used **TO WIPE THEIR BEHINDS:** rose petals, leaves, straw, rags, pages from catalogues or books, corncobs.

LEECHES have been used in *medicine* for more than **3,000 years.**

Leeches were put over an affected area to suck out "bad" blood.

During the 1830s in France, more than 35 million leeches were used in medicinal treatments PER YEAR!

Once a Parisian leech collector fell asleep and woke up to find himself completely covered in leeches!

But I LIKE my HEAD!

KING CHARLES I

was BEHEADED for being a traitor.

Out of RESPECT for the royal family, his head was later SEWN BACK ON.

Thank you. THAT'S MUCH BETTER.

KING LOUIS XIII

of France suffered from BALDNESS, so he started a trend of wearing BIG, CURLY WIGS.

The trend spread to **CHARLES II**, the king of England at the time.

It is still common for **JUDGES** in England to wear **WIGS**.

JAPANESE **SAMURAI** had **SOCKS** with a **SEPARATE PLACE** for the **BIG TOES.**

The average SAMURAI stood only about 1.63 METRES (5 FEET, 4 INCHES) TALL.

SAMURAI were trained in BATTLE TACTICS, SWORDSMANSHIP and POETRY.

VIKINGS bathed about ONCE A WEEK – way more OFTEN than most PEOPLE OF THE DAY.

What did Vikings do for fun? THEY SKIED!

Contrary to popular belief, **VIKINGS** DID NOT WEAR HORNS on their helmets.

To navigate the ocean, **VIKINGS** used **CRYSTALS.**

VIKINGS buried their dead in boats.

THE RMS *TITANIC*

The *TITANIC'S ANCHOR* weighed more than 14 metric tons (15 tons). **TWENTY HORSES HAD TO CARRY IT TO THE SHIPYARD!**

The last
meal for the
Titanic's first class
passengers
included
11 COURSES!

After the
Titanic sank,
ROWS OF
UNBROKEN
CHINA PLATES
rested on the
ocean floor.

ESSEX

In 1820 the 216-metric ton (238-ton) whaling ship **ESSEX** capsized after being rammed twice by a **SPERM WHALE**.

The **FEW SURVIVORS** drifted on the sea in small boats for 94 **DAYS BEFORE BEING RESCUED.**

Herman Melville's novel *MOBY DICK* was inspired by the harrowing tale.

HINDENBURG

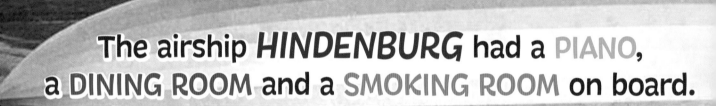

The airship **HINDENBURG** had a PIANO,
a DINING ROOM and a SMOKING ROOM on board.

AIRSHIPS, INCLUDING THE *HINDENBURG*, WERE ABOUT 229–244 METRES (750–800 FEET) LONG. THAT'S ABOUT AS LONG AS 2 ½ FOOTBALL FIELDS.

D-LZ129

The *Hindenburg* **EXPLODED** in 1937. No one knows why.

COOL JOBS OF THE PAST

A **RESURRECTIONIST** snatched bodies from graves and sold them to medical schools.

When digging a body from a grave, a **RESURRECTIONIST** used a **WOODEN SHOVEL** so it wouldn't make any noise.

BODY SNATCHING was so common in the 17th century that people started to bury their dead in metal, cage-like caskets.

MORE COOL JOBS

KNOCKER-UPPERS tapped on windows with large poles or shot peas out of straws to wake up factory workers.

THE GROOM OF THE STOOL wiped a king's behind after he used the toilet.

A **DOG WHIPPER** kept dogs quiet in the churchyard.

ROYAL RAT CATCHERS CAUGHT RATS.
Rat Catcher John Newton could catch up to
340 RATS in one night at Windsor Castle!

If you lived in the 17th century and you wanted to insult a **man's intelligence** you would call him a

"wattlehead".

Throughout history, **LAZY PEOPLE** have been called

BED-PRESSERS, LOLL-POOPS AND LOITERSACKS.

THE AMERICAN WORD "POOP" WAS NOT USED UNTIL AROUND 1900.

INSTEAD OF "POO" THE BRITISH USED:

NIGHT SOIL – poo removed from European cities at night

GONG – a historical word for poo

THREE THINGS
most **SEA-FARING COLONISTS**
had in common:

HEAD LICE

BIG DREAMS

BODY LICE

KRISTI YAMAGUCHI, 1992 Olympic gold medallist figure skater, was born with **DEFORMED FEET**.

After contracting POLIO as a child and spending YEARS IN A LEG BRACE, **WILMA RUDOLPH** went on to win THREE GOLD MEDALS in track and field in the 1960 OLYMPICS.

South African swimmer **NATALIE DU TOIT** competed in the 2008 Beijing Olympics with an AMPUTATED LEG AND NO PROSTHESIS.

LONGEST TENNIS MATCH:

11 hours over a stretch of 3 days
THEY PLAYED 183 GAMES IN TOTAL!
(Isner vs. Mahut, 2010)

THE LONGEST BASKETBALL GAME

HAD SIX OVERTIME PERIODS!

Indianapolis Olympians
vs.
Rochester Royals, 1951

Romanian president *Nicolae Ceaușescu* banned the board game

SCRABBLE.

In 2011 the Malaysian government banned people from wearing YELLOW.

Since 1992 it has been illegal to chew **GUM** in Singapore.

For over 200 years, it was illegal in France for women to wear TROUSERS in public.

In 2012 **KING RICHARD III**'s body was found under a car park in England.

From the 16th to 19th centuries, **DECEASED MONKS IN PALERMO, ITALY,** were mummified, dressed and put on display.

Today, tourists can visit the Palermo, Italy, monks at the Catacombs of the Capuchins.

THE INCA PEOPLE

from South America used **LLAMA DUNG** for fuel.

EARLY AMERICAN PIONEERS

burned dried buffalo poo to keep warm.

PIANO KEYS

were once made from elephant and walrus tusks.

In the 1800s, **WHALE PARTS** were used to make **CORSETS.**

The Catholic Pope **LEO X** had a pet **WHITE ELEPHANT** named Hanno.

Napoleon's wife had a **PET ORANGUTAN** that enjoyed dining on turnips.

The Spanish artist **SALVADOR DALÌ** would take his pet ocelot, **BABOU**, out to eat.

93

MOZART

held a FUNERAL
when his
PET BIRD died.

US president **ANDREW JACKSON** loved his **PARROT** so much that it was invited to his **FUNERAL**.

A mythical
triangle called the

BERMUDA TRIANGLE

covers more than
1,294,994 square kilometres
(500,00 square miles)
of ocean just off the
southeastern coast
of Florida.

More than
100 STRANGE HAPPENINGS
have been reported in the
BERMUDA TRIANGLE.

On 5 December 1945,
five US Navy bombers
VANISHED INTO THIN AIR
over the BERMUDA TRIANGLE.

In 1924 a **CAR** in the United States **COST ABOUT £200.00.**

£200.00

THE FIRST SEATBELTS

were not put into
cars until the 1950s.

Car seats for babies were not
widely used in the United Kingdom
until the 1980s.

THE FIRST COMPUTERS WERE GIGANTIC. THEY OFTEN FILLED ENTIRE ROOMS!

The first **COMPUTER MOUSE** had a wooden shell and two wheels.

THE APOLLO 11 MISSION USED COMPUTERS less powerful than your MOBILE PHONE!

The first
KENTUCKY FRIED CHICKEN
restaurant was
inside a
PETROL STATION.

TACO BELL – today
a billion-pound
business – started
out as a
HOT DOG
STAND.

The first **McDonald's** restaurant served peanut butter and jam **sandwiches.**

THE FIRST HOLLYWOOD FILM (made in 1910) only took **TWO DAYS** to shoot.

In the 1970s film *THE SWARM,* the studio used **22 MILLION LIVE BEES.**

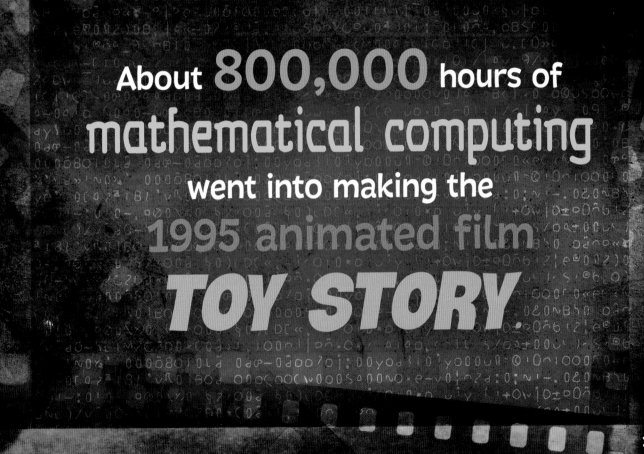

About 800,000 hours of **mathematical computing** went into making the 1995 animated film **TOY STORY**

THE TATOOINE SCENES

in the **STAR WARS** movies were filmed in Tunisia, Africa.

If you visit **TUNISIA,** you can actually stay in **LUKE SKYWALKER'S** home. It's a **HOTEL** now.

In 1967 Canada built a

UFO LANDING PAD

TO WELCOME ALIENS. So far NO ALIENS HAVE USED IT.

GLOSSARY

aviation having to do with the flying, development or the business of aircraft

capsize when a boat turns over in the water

ceasefire stop fighting a war for a specific period of time

decree official order

descendant person related to someone from the past

pioneer person who is among the first to do something

polio disease that affects the nerves; it often makes people unable to walk

president in some places in the world, a president is the head of government

propeller group of blades that, when spinning, help an aircraft to fly

samurai warrior from Japan

READ MORE

The Usborne Book of Famous Artists, Various (Usborne Publishing, 2014)

The Usborne Medieval World (World History), Jane Bingham (Usborne Publishing, 2015)

Vikings (Eyewonder), DK (DK Children, 2016)

World War I (Tony Robinson's Weird World of Wonders), Sir Tony Robinson (Macmillan Children's Books, 2013)

WEBSITES

www.bbc.co.uk/education/topics/ztyr9j6
Watch animated clips about Viking life at this BBC website.

www.iwm.org.uk/history/learning-resources
Learn more about World War I at the Imperial War Museum's official website.

www.sciencemuseum.org.uk/broughttolife/people
Learn about famous and important people throughout history via this interactive timeline from the Science Museum.

INDEX

Raintree is an imprint of Capstone Global Library Limited,
a company incorporated in England and Wales having its registered office at
264 Banbury Road, Oxford, OX2 7DY – Registered company number: 6695582

www.raintree.co.uk
myorders@raintree.co.uk

Text © Capstone Global Library Limited 2017
The moral rights of the proprietor have been asserted.

Editor: Megan Atwood | Designer: Veronica Scott | Media Researcher: Jo Miller | Production Specialist: Gene Bentdahl

ISBN 978 1 4747 1289 7 (hardback)
20 19 18 17 16
10 9 8 7 6 5 4 3 2 1

British Library Cataloguing in Publication Data
A full catalogue record for this book is available from the British Library.

Acknowledgements
We would like to thank the following for permission to reproduce photographs:
Alamy: Chronicle, 30, dieKleinert, 97, INTERFOTO, 67, North Wind Picture Archives, 3; AP Images: Alastair Grant, File, 82, (front); Bridgeman Images: Private Collection/Photo © O. Vaering, 61, Corbis: Jason Hawkes, 73, (castle), Underwood & Underwood, 24, (Woodrow Wilson); Getty Images: Bettmann, 7, Hulton Archive/Three Lions/Lucien Aigner, 18, 19, Print Collector/Ann Ronan Pictures, 23; Newscom: akg-images, 58, 79, 95 (Andrew Jackson), akg-images/Andre Held, 34, Cultura/George Karbus Photography, 66, Design Pics, 35, (right), Design Pics/Steve Nagy, 108-109, Everett Collection, 10, 80, (right), 91, 93, 98, 103, Florilegius/Album, 33, (left), Glasshouse Images/Manning de V. Lee, 62, Icon SMI/Manny Millan, 80, (left), Ingram Publishing, 84, REX/Mark Pain, 81, UIG National Trust, 54, 55, 57, (left), World History Archive, (left), 68-69, (airship), ZUMA Press/Glen Stubbe, 45, ZUMA Press/Mark Richards, 100, ZUMA Press/Ropi/Antonio Pisacreta, 87; Shutterstock: Adwo, 15, albund, 82, (background), 49, (pie), Algol, 63, Amy Johansson, 28 (plank), Andrey_Kuzmin, 29, (porthole), Art Konovalov, 9, Asaf Eliason, 11 (both), bikeriderlondon, 36-37, camilla$$, back cover, Christos Georghiou, 101, Creative Travel Projects, 24, (background), cynoclub, 95 (parrot), dedMazay, 70, Dobrynina Elena, 42, Eka Panova, 31 (all), Elle Arden Images, 12, Eric Isselee, 43, Everett Historical, cover (tank), 2, 8, 13, 16, 27, 29, (pirate), 38, 40, 64, exopixel, 51, (corn cob), Georgios Kollidas, 44, GreenBelka, 96, gst, 102, (left), jaylopez, 105, Joshua Rainey Photography, 88, Kristen Smith, 32, (left), Lena_graphics, cover, (alien), Lightspring, 83, Luca Nichetti, 49, (bird), Magdanatka, 51, (rose petals), Marques, 106-107, Marzolino, 20, Marzolino, 32, (right), Oliver Hoffmann, 102, (right), PathDoc, 74, PathDoc, 75, patrimonio designs ltd, cover, (samurai), Pelevina Ksinia, 73, (rat), PhotoTodos, 51, (book), Protasov AN, 78, 79, scimmery, 5, Sergiu Ungureanu, 24, (golf ball), sharpner, 57, (right), Studio_smile, 28-29, Sudowoodo, cover, (poop), Sudowoodo, 76, 77, sydeen, 52, TaMaNKunG, 39, (background), The_Pixel, 68-69, (football fields), vasosh, 39, (soccer ball), vitmark, 88-89, Wallenrock, 4, SuperStock: Science and Society, 71, Wikimedia: Carlo Crivelli, 33, (right)

Design Elements by Capstone and Shutterstock

Printed and bound in China.